Silly Sketcher

Draw Bobbleheads!

written by Luke Colins

illustrated by Catherine Cates

BLACK
RABBIT
BOOKS

Hi Jinx is published by Black Rabbit Books
P.O. Box 3263, Mankato, Minnesota, 56002.
www.blackrabbitbooks.com
Copyright © 2019 Black Rabbit Books

Jennifer Besel, editor; Michael Sellner and Catherine Cates, designers; Omay Ayres, photo researcher

All rights reserved. No part of this book may be reproduced in any form without written permission from the publisher.

Library of Congress Cataloging-in-Publication Data
Names: Colins, Luke, author.
Title: Draw bobbleheads! / by Luke Colins.
Description: Mankato, Minnesota : Black Rabbit Books, 2019. | Series: Hi jinx. Silly sketcher | Includes bibliographical references and index. | Audience: Ages 9-12. | Audience: Grades 4 to 6. Identifiers: LCCN 2017061825 (print) | LCCN 2018005912 (ebook) | ISBN 9781680726046 (e-book) | ISBN 9781680725988 (library binding) | ISBN 9781680727463 (pbk.)
Subjects: LCSH: Cartoon characters—Juvenile literature. | Cartooning—Technique—Juvenile literature.
Classification: LCC NC1764 (ebook) | LCC NC1764 .C65 2019 (print) | DDC 741.5/1—dc23
LC record available at https://lccn.loc.gov/2017061825

Printed in the United States. 4/18

Image Credits

Alamy: Matthew Cole, 5 (markers); iStock: carbouval, 5 (sharpener & eraser); doodlemachine, 20 (cartoons); Shutterstock: designer_an, 19 (waves bkgd); Mario Pantelic, Cover, Back Cover, 1, 3, 5, 12 (line doodle bkgd); Memo Angeles, Cover (boy & pencil), 4 (donkey & monster), 5 (pencil, kids & hands), 6 (girl), 8 (boy), 11 (boy), 13 (girl), 16 (girl), 18 (girl), 20 (boy), 23 (boy & pencil); Mochipet, 11 (flags); Olga Sabo, 2–3, 5 (colored pencils); opicobello, 7 (torn paper), 11 (marker strokes), 17 (torn paper); owatta, 5 (paper); Pasko Maksim, Back Cover, 12, 23, 24 (torn paper); Pitju, 3, 8, 21 (curled corner); Ron Dale, 3, 4, 5, 6, 7, 11, 12, 17, 20 (marker stroke)
Every effort has been made to contact copyright holders for material reproduced in this book. Any omissions will be rectified in subsequent printings if notice is given to the publisher.

Contents

CHAPTER 1
Be a Silly Sketcher!.....4

CHAPTER 2
Put Your Pencil to
the Paper............6

CHAPTER 3
Get in on the Hi Jinx...20

Other Resources............22

Chapter 1
Be a Silly Sketcher!

Big heads on tiny bodies are hilarious! And they're even funnier when you draw them yourself. Pair art and humor with these fun bobblehead drawings.

To be a silly sketcher, all you need is a pencil, some paper, and a funny bone. Use an oval here. Put a line there. Just follow the steps. You'll have everyone laughing with your drawings in no time.

What You Need

pencils

pencil sharpener
(just in case)

lots of paper

eraser

colored pencils and markers

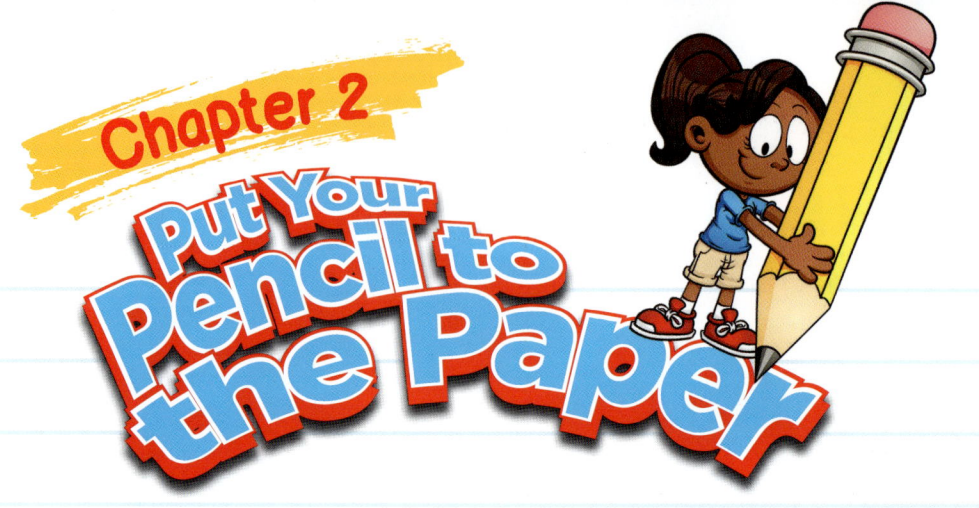

Chapter 2
Put Your Pencil to the Paper

The laughter will snowball out of control with this silly snowman sketch.

Step 1
Draw a large circle. Then draw a small circle above it. Then draw a medium-sized circle above that.

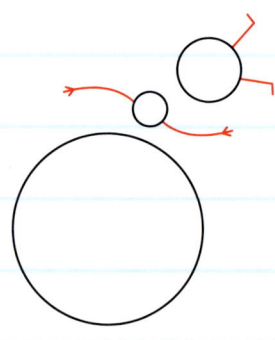

Step 2
Use wavy lines to add arms to the small circle. Use straight lines to put legs on the medium circle.

Step 3
Add two big eye circles **overlapping** the large circle. Draw **motion** lines next to the eyes. Then sketch in some tiny circles around the body.

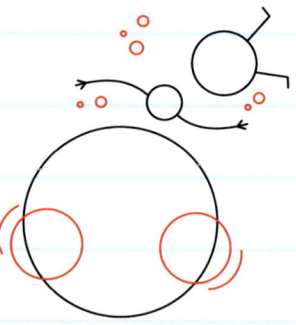

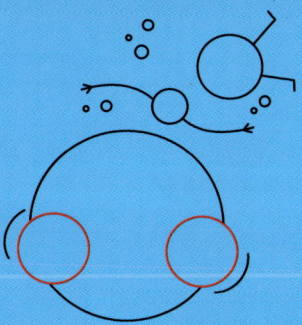

Step 4
Erase all the lines inside the overlapping circles.

Step 5
Give your snowman a funny face, complete with a carrot nose.

Step 6
Add button details and a small hat.

Step 7
Put in some fun motion lines to make your falling snowman even sillier.

Finish It Up!
Use markers to **outline** your drawing. Then try colored pencils for shading it in.

Rainy Day Cat

Yes, cats can make purrr-fect bobbleheads!

Step 1
Draw a curved rectangle with two points at each end.

Step 2
Make a teardrop shape for the head. But at the top, draw an opening to create ears. Also add a fun little tail.

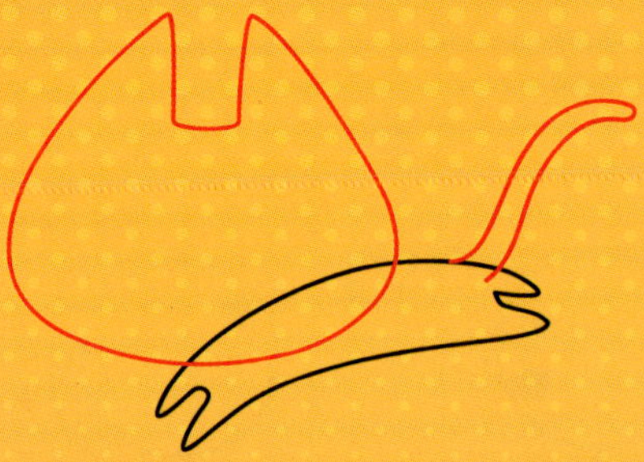

Step 3
Erase all the lines inside the overlapping shapes.

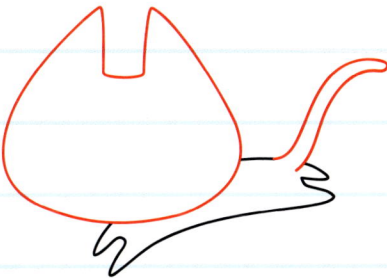

Step 4
Give your cat big eyes, whiskers, and a mouth.

Step 5
Add fun boots to the cat's feet.

Step 6
Erase the lines inside the boots.

Step 7
Use a half-circle shape and curved lines to draw an umbrella. Use a J shape for the handle.

Step 8
Draw raindrops and wind lines to finish the picture.

Abraham Bobblehead

You don't need to **compliment** this former president to give him a big head. Just draw him one!

Step 1
Draw a tall rectangle on your paper. Then add two straight lines across the middle.

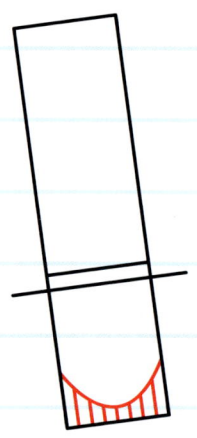

Step 2
Add a curved line near the bottom of the rectangle. Fill in the space with short straight lines.

Step 3
Put on a face with eyes, a nose, and a mouth. Don't forget the eyebrows!

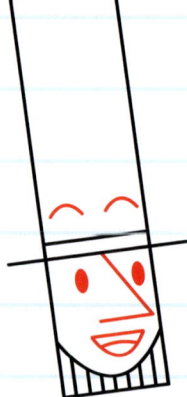

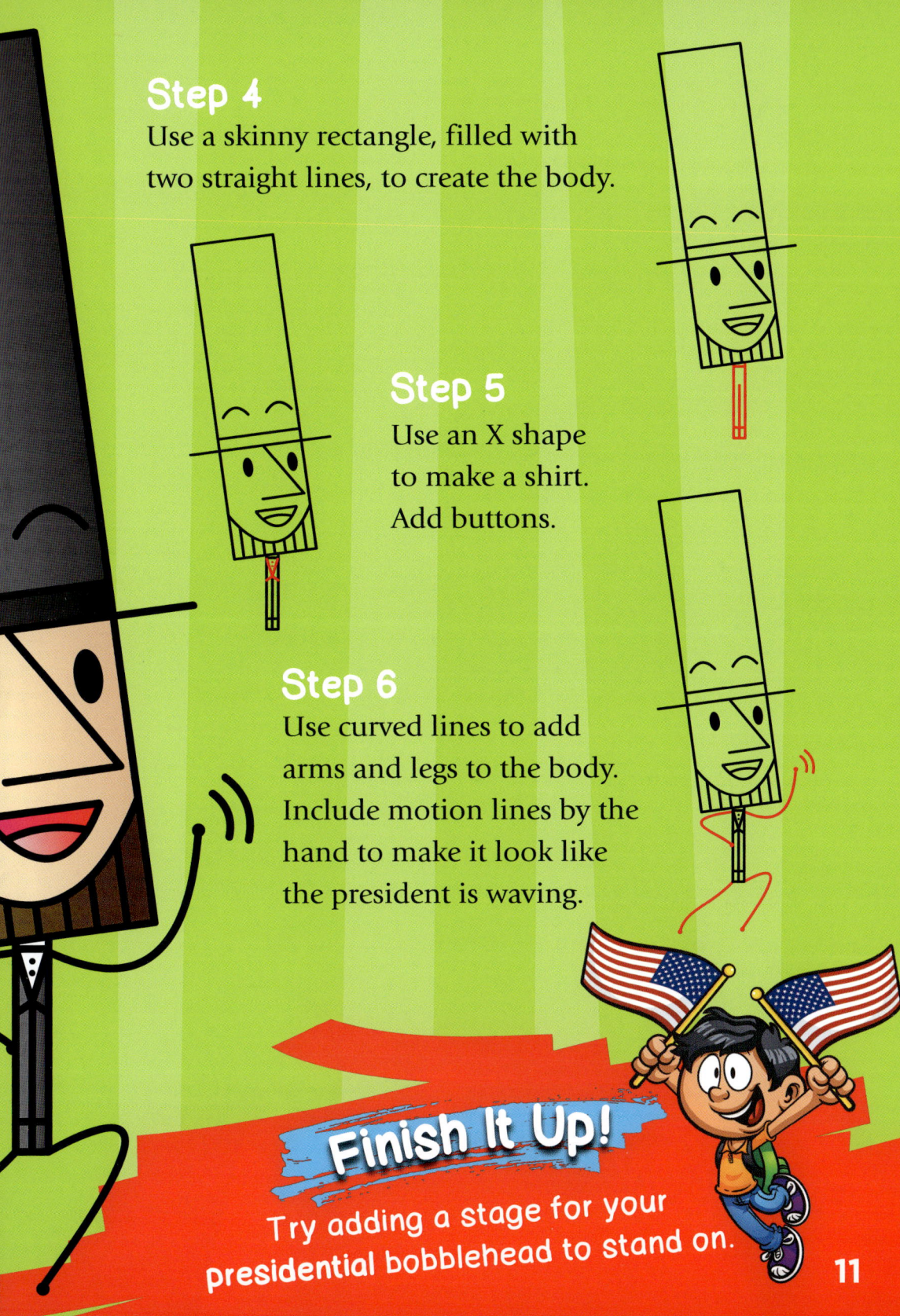

Step 4
Use a skinny rectangle, filled with two straight lines, to create the body.

Step 5
Use an X shape to make a shirt. Add buttons.

Step 6
Use curved lines to add arms and legs to the body. Include motion lines by the hand to make it look like the president is waving.

Finish It Up!
Try adding a stage for your presidential bobblehead to stand on.

High-Kicking Ninja

Feeling sneaky? Try your hand at this big-headed ninja. Draw quietly because that's what a ninja would do.

Step 1
Start the body by drawing two triangles with the points touching.

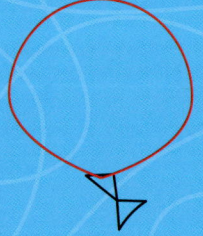

Step 2
Add a big circle above the triangles.

Step 3
Add a mask shape inside the circle.

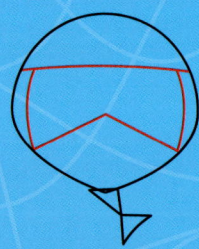

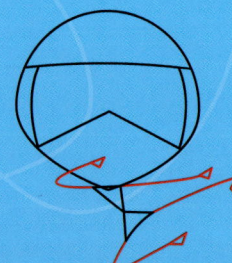

Step 4
Draw curved lines for arms and legs. Use small triangles for the hands and feet.

Finish It Up!
Color your ninja however you'd like. Not all ninjas have to dress in black.

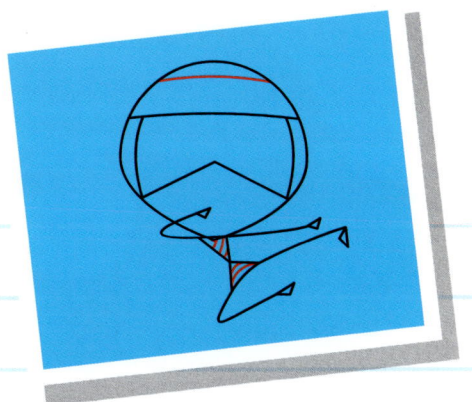

Step 5
Add detail lines at the top of the head and inside the body.

Step 6
Give the ninja a face with big eyes, **diagonal** eyebrows, and a straight mouth.

Step 7
Give the ninja a belt. Erase any overlapping lines. Finally, add a big S shape to show how fast your ninja moves.

Wild Wizard

This bobblehead starts with a few simple shapes. It'll seem like magic when this drawing comes together.

Step 1
Use straight and curved lines to start the wizard's body.

Step 2

Draw a big teardrop shape on its side for a head. Then add arms and little hands.

Step 3
Use straight lines to add sleeves. Then add another curved line to finish the wizard's robe.

Step 4
Give your wizard a big eye, tiny nose, and smiling mouth. Add a wand in one hand too.

Step 5
Use jagged lines to give the wizard some crazy hair.

Step 6
Add a fun hat to your drawing.

Step 7
Erase all the lines inside the overlapping shapes.

Step 8
Add details to your drawing, such as a tongue and eyebrow. Give the wand a little magic too.

Cursed King Tut

King Tut's tomb might be **cursed**. But your drawing won't be.

Step 1
Draw an upside-down **pentagon**.

Step 2
Draw a half oval around the pentagon. Then add two skinny triangles on the bottom.

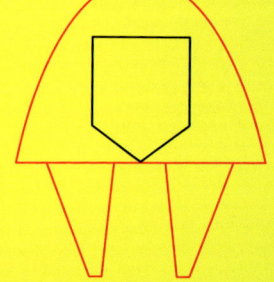

Step 3
Use straight and curved lines to add details to the king's hat.

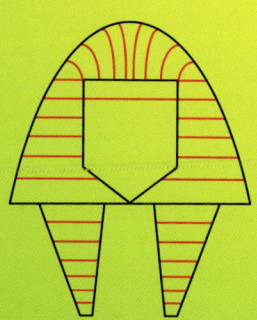

Step 4
Add small triangles to the top and bottom of the hat.

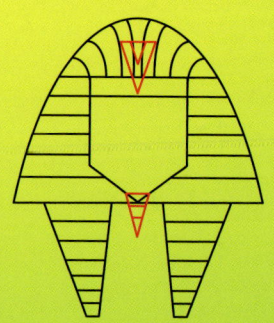

Step 5
Erase all the lines inside the overlapping shapes.

Step 6
Draw a second triangle around the one at the bottom of the hat. Then add a skinny rectangle with detail lines.

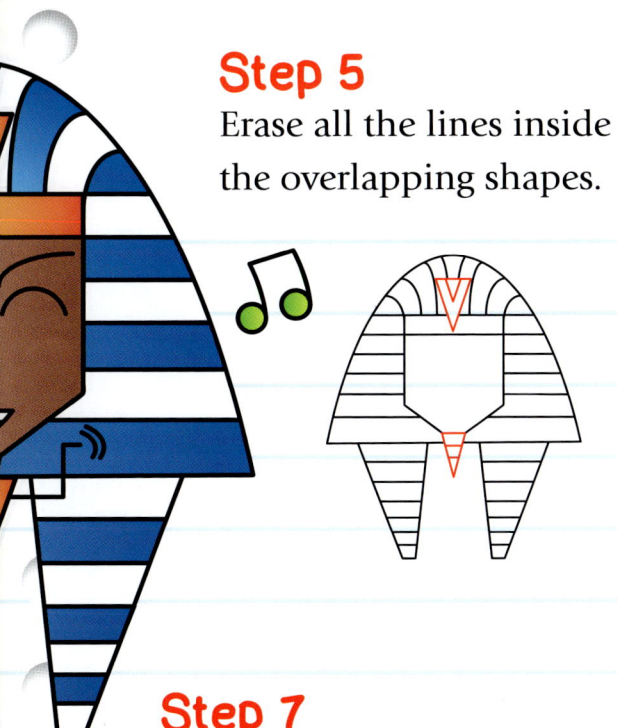

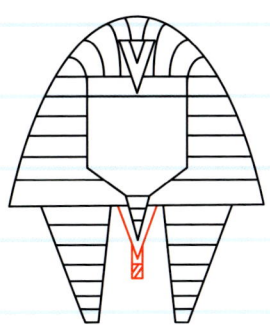

Step 7
Use straight lines to add arms and legs. Put motion lines by the arms to make the king dance.

Step 8
Give the king a happy face. Add some musical notes too.

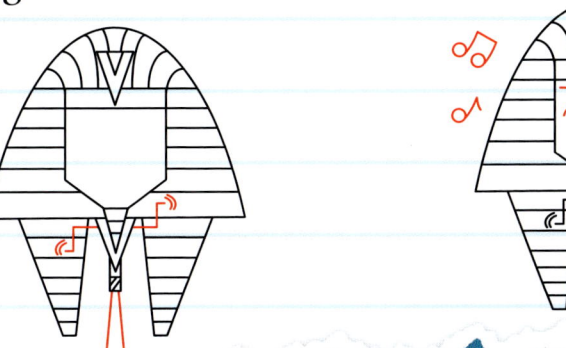

Tip
Your King Tut doesn't have to dance. Instead of musical notes, use other details to set the scene.

Diving Koala

What's funnier than a koala on a diving board? Try a big-headed koala on a diving board!

Step 1
Draw a big circle on your page. Then add a skinny teardrop shape underneath.

Step 2
Add a small, rounded triangle overlapping the circle and teardrop. These will be hands. Put a T shape at the bottom of the teardrop for feet.

Step 3
Use straight lines to add detail to the body.

Step 4

Add large, rounded ears on the sides of the circle. Use jagged lines to add fur.

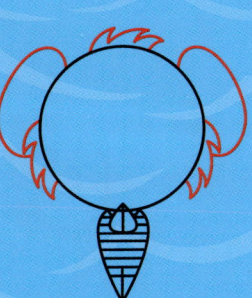

Step 5

Give your koala a fun face.

Step 6

Use rectangles to draw a diving board.

Step 7

Draw in a ladder up to the board. Add motion lines to show how high the koala can jump.

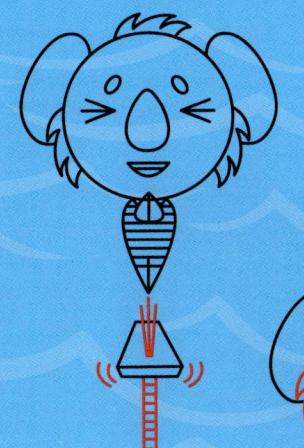

Step 8

Erase all the lines inside the overlapping shapes.

Chapter 3
Get in on the Hi Jinx

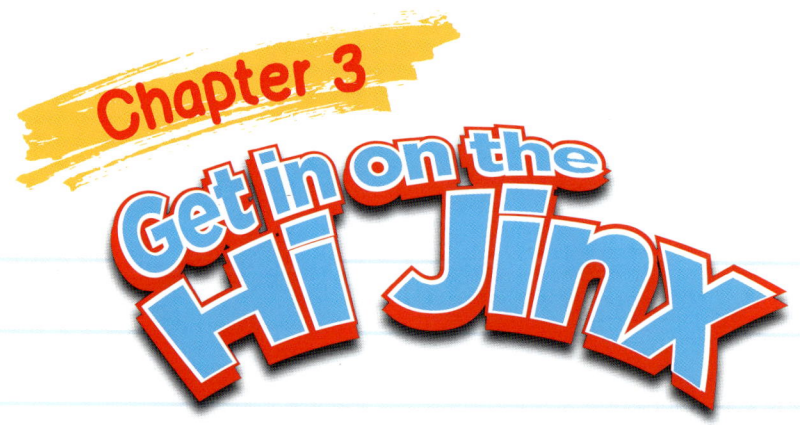

Cartoon artists use the same steps you just did! They use simple shapes to build the frames of their drawings. Then they put on **exaggerated** features to add humor. Maybe you'll be a cartoon artist one day.

Take It One Step More

1. Why is it important to erase the lines inside other lines?

2. Are your sketches more or less funny with color? Why?

3. What features make these drawings funny?

GLOSSARY

compliment (KOM-pluh-ment)—an expression of respect or admiration

cursed (KURSD)—to be under an evil spell meant to cause harm

diagonal (dy-AG-nuhl)—running in a slanted direction

exaggerated (ig-ZAH-juh-ray-tyd)—enlarged beyond the normal bounds or beyond the truth

motion (MO-shun)—an act or process of moving

outline (AHWT-lyn)—to draw a line around the edges of something

overlap (oh-vur-LAP)—to extend over or past

pentagon (PEN-tuh-gahn)—a shape with five sides and five angles

presidential (prez-uh-DEN-shul)—having the qualities of a high-level leader

LEARN MORE

BOOKS

Antram, David. *Caricatures.* Step-by-Step Draw. Mankato, MN: Book House, 2017.

Beaumont, Steve. *How to Draw Weird Fantasy Art.* Creating Fantasy Art. New York: Rosen, 2018.

Johnson, Clare. *How to Draw.* New York: Dorling Kindersley Limited, 2017.

WEBSITES

Drawing for Kids
mocomi.com/fun/arts-crafts/drawing-for-kids/

Drawing for Kids
www.hellokids.com/r_12/drawing-for-kids/

How to Draw for Kids
www.artforkidshub.com/how-to-draw/

TIPS AND TRICKS

Make sure to let the marker outlines dry before coloring in your drawings.

Colored pencils are a great tool for coloring in your drawings. Layer one color over another for a cool blended effect.

Can't draw a straight line? Try using a ruler or other straight edge.

Don't worry if your drawings don't look exactly like the ones in this book! Art is all about creating your own thing. Just have fun!